GOD AT WORK

COURSE

Living every day with purpose

LEADERS' GUIDE

CONTENTS

PREFACE

'During the last thirty years, being a Christian at work has, if anything, become more difficult. Markets have become volatile, decisions more complex and few choices are clear-cut. Within this context, finding purpose at work is one of the greatest challenges in the globalised world today. This course is full of practical tools that I have personally found helpful during 30 years of work in the city. It aims to help you discover the God-given purpose that you have in your work and to equip you to live it out with integrity. I hope that from my own experience of hardship and joy in the workplace, you may catch some glimpse of God at work, and that he may help you as he has helped me.'

Ken Costa

ENDORSEMENTS

'No one is better qualified than Ken Costa to write a course like this. Throughout his rise to one of the most senior positions in the banking world, he has been an inspiration to countless Christians seeking to live out their faith in their workplaces. Ken and I met at Cambridge University where we both became Christians. He has been one of my closest friends ever since. I am so glad he has been persuaded at last to put some of his wisdom and experience into print.'

Nicky Gumbel
Vicar of Holy Trinity Brompton, London
Pioneer of the Alpha course

'My friend, Ken Costa, shares practical and life changing steps to live out your faith at work.'

Rick Warren
Pastor and Author of the International Bestseller, 'The Purpose Driven Life'

'Brilliantly written and structured by someone who has had years of experience in high pressure work place environments.'

Rohan Karat
Deutsche Bank

'The course went down really well when we used it in the workplace and the HR department advertised it as they felt it would be of benefit to a much wider audience. It is easy to use, profound in its application and made a deep impact in many of the guests' lives. One guest said "I wished I'd done this course 25 years ago!"'

Ric Thorpe
Course Leader, News International

'I had the privilege of participating in a *God at Work* course. The topics included ethical decision-making, personality conflicts, and money, amongst others. Our conversations were always interesting, thought-provoking, and inspiring. Anyone who has held a job has faced some of the situations that we considered. I would highly recommend attending the course if you are interested in examining God's presence in your workplace.'

Shelley Manson
Course Attendee

'I found the God at Work course to be very encouraging and enlightening. It provides thought provoking questions that lead to reflection on how we interact with others, align our values with our work, and ultimately how we choose to serve. I would highly recommend it to anyone who wants to reflect on their life purpose.'

Alanna Donahue
Director of Philanthropy at BC Children's Hospital Foundation

INTRODUCTION

WHO IS THE COURSE FOR?

The material is aimed at both Christians and those still exploring their faith. The material is relevant to everyone, in the sense that we all 'work' in one way or another, whether we are currently employed or whether we plan to work in the future. The course is aimed at:

- those in paid employment

- those working in the voluntary sector

- those who work but are not paid (eg, stay-at-home parents)

- those who are between jobs

- those currently not working, but who hope to work in the future (eg, students)

WHERE CAN THE COURSE BE USED?

God at Work is a six-session course that can be used in a variety of settings, from church small groups and mid-sized communities to workplace fellowships.

WHAT IS THE AIM OF THE COURSE?

Finding purpose in the work we do is one of the greatest challenges we face. The *God at Work* course aims to equip Christians to live out their Christian calling at work and find purpose in every aspect of their working lives. The course provides a Christian perspective on how to face challenges at work, as well as teaching on how to support our family and friends in the difficulties we all inevitably face.

THINGS TO DO BEFORE YOUR GOD AT WORK COURSE STARTS

1. Read Ken Costa's book *God at Work*

2. Pray:
   - that many guests will register, including people who may be struggling with the issues that are covered on the course
   - for all of the course logistics
   - that everything will run smoothly, and no unforseen obstacles will present themselves

3. Plan the course – carefully look into dates, times and locations that work for the guests that you are trying to attract. Plan how you are going to invite people to join you; remember a personal invitation often works best!

4. Once everything is in place, please **register your course online** at www.godatwork.org.uk
   This helps us to support you and allows potential guests to find out about your course

5. Invite the guests

6. Go for it and keep praying

7. Listen to the course podcasts online at godatwork.org.uk/podcast
   It is best to listen to the relevant podcast as you prepare for each respective session, so that the information is fresh in your mind before you lead

8. At the end of the course we would love to hear your **feedback** on how it went: how many people attended, what worked well and what didn't work so well, etc

Practical Details

FORMAT

Each of the six sessions includes teaching from the course leader, group discussion, testimonies and additional homework exercises. The group discussion should take place in small groups of between three and six people, and for consistency you may wish to keep the same groups throughout the course. If the course is being held with a larger group it would be beneficial to have a time of worship at the start of each session.

TIMINGS

The course is divided into six sessions and may be given as a series over six weeks, or longer, depending on your individual situation. Each session lasts approximately an hour, although the timings can be adjusted to allow more or less time if necessary.

MATERIALS REQUIRED

To run the course successfully you will need:

- a copy of this leaders' guide
- a guest manual for each guest

It may be also helpful to have a copy of the book *God at Work*, by Ken Costa (Continuum, 2007).

The leader should read through the above and become familiar with the material before beginning the course.

WHO SHOULD LEAD THE COURSE?

THE TEACHING

The teaching sessions should be presented by a leader who is familiar with the material, and preferably someone who is also passionate about equipping Christians to be effective in their work. It is preferable if the small group leader is able to bring their own experience of work into the sessions.

In some situations it may be beneficial to use different leaders for the sessions to benefit from the experience of a variety of people. Session 1 covers the theology of work and it is therefore recommended that this session is given by someone who has a good understanding of the theology, thus allowing them to answer any questions, or give further explanation if required.

TESTIMONIES

Most sessions also include story or testimony slots. These are opportunities to show how the material in the book works in practice, by hearing from individuals who have applied the teaching to their own work situations. If you are giving the session you may have a personal example to share. Alternatively, you could ask someone from your group to share their own experience. It is worth asking around to find people who can do this before the course begins, briefing them on what they should say in advance. The person speaking should talk for no longer than five minutes; it is a good idea to ensure that you have heard their story before asking them to speak! Choose speakers whom you respect, and whom you believe can inspire others. The session outlines include sample stories from the *God at Work* book that can be used if you cannot find someone to give a live testimony.

SESSION 1

Work Matters

PREPARE BEFOREHAND

- If you haven't done so already, please register your course online at godatwork.org.uk
- Before preparing their own talks, leaders can listen to a podcast of Ken Costa discussing the content of this session in an interview with Nicky Gumbel. For a full list of podcasts, please visit godatwork.org.uk/podcast
- Bring a copy of the *God at Work* book to show
- Testimony slot – ask someone to share their own experience of discerning God's purpose for their work (or give this example from your own life)
- Take a few minutes at the start of this first session to explain the format the course will take and any additional arrangements (small group format, etc)

WELCOME AND INTRODUCTION

Welcome to the first session of *God at Work*. You may be wondering why you are here, or what you can hope to learn from doing a course like this.

The material is aimed at Christians at any stage of faith, as well as those who are still exploring. The material is relevant to everyone, in the sense that we all 'work' in one way or another, whether we are currently employed or whether we plan to work in the future. The course is aimed at:

- those in paid employment
- those working in the voluntary sector
- those who work but are not paid (eg, stay-at-home parents)
- those who are between jobs
- those currently not working, but who hope to work in the future (eg, students)

Finding purpose in our work is one of the greatest challenges we face. The *God at Work* course aims to equip Christians to live out their God-given calling at work, and find purpose in every aspect of their working lives, no matter what form that may take. The course provides a Christian perspective on how to face challenges at work, as well as teaching on how we can best support our family and friends in the difficulties we all inevitably face.

The course is based on the book *God at Work*, by Ken Costa. Ken is Chairman of the investment bank Lazard International, and has been a banker in the city of London for over thirty years. He is also Chairman of Alpha International and Church Warden at Holy Trinity Brompton Church in London. He is married to Fi and they have four children. Clearly, Ken has known the pressure of maintaining work and family life!

Why do we need Christian teaching about work?

Many Christians see their work as part of their Christian calling, but most feel poorly equipped to live out this calling. This course aims to readdress the balance, by looking at six key areas that are relevant to our working lives. They are:

1. Work Matters
2. Ambition and Life Choices
3. Tough Decisions
4. Stress and Work-Life Balance
5. Failure, Disappointment and Hope
6. Money and Giving

WHY IS THE COURSE RELEVANT FOR YOU?

In response to the question, 'What does God do all day?' John Ortberg writes in his book, *If You Want to Walk on Water, You've Got to Get Out of the Boat*, (Zondervan, 2003):

'The biblical writers tell us what God does in a single phrase: He works.'

Throughout scripture, God is described as:

- a gardener
- an artist
- a potter
- a shepherd
- a king
- a home-maker
- a builder

The psalmist declares 'O Lord, how manifold are your works!' (Psalm 104:24, American KJV).

'Jesus said to them, "My Father is always at his work to this very day, and I, too, am working"' (John 5:17).

In other words, God works!

We are made in the image of God, and therefore each of us is made to work, whether we are paid for it or not.

EXERCISE 1 – IN SMALL GROUPS (5 MINS)

Ask the guests to get into their small groups and to go around quickly telling each other what they do for work. This doesn't need to be a long explanation. Eg, 'I work as a nurse at a children's hospital', 'I am an accountant who works at a big firm in the city' or, 'I am a stay-at-home mum looking after our two children'.

Then, discuss the following question in small groups:

What might prevent a Christian from taking their faith into the workplace?

At the end of the discussion ask the groups to feed back their answers. The key reasons to highlight are:

- fear
- the sacred/secular divide in society
- having no 'model' for what 'being a Christian at work' might look like
- being unaware of the spiritual battle that rages in the workplace
- not believing that our work has inherent value in God's sight

We will only take our faith into the workplace if we believe that our work is valuable to God.

STARTING POINTS FOR A THEOLOGICAL UNDERSTANDING OF WORK

To start, we're going to explore the theology of work. What does a biblical view of work look like?

1. THE TRINITY

Work invariably involves working with other people. This can either be the most rewarding part of our job, or the most difficult, dependent upon the quality of relationships we have with our colleagues.

We need look no further than the Trinity to find the ultimate model of loving teamwork. In Genesis 1 we read about the Creation of the world and we find the three members of the Trinity working together – the Father creates through speaking, the Son is his Word, and the Spirit is there, hovering above the waters (Genesis 1:2).

Our model for corporate life essentially stems from this model of teamwork.

Who do we serve at work?

Ask for responses from the guests – they may vary!

Work is, at the most fundamental level, about service. When we work, we are serving either our own interests, those of others (our employers), or God. The root motivation for effective service is love.

The love between the members of the Trinity – Father, Son and Holy Spirit – should act as the ultimate model for teamwork.

2. CREATION

Looking at Creation helps us to understand the biblical structure for work on a number of levels.

First, we have the precedent of God himself working to create the world. God works for six days and then rests on the seventh. As we are created in God's image, we should do the same.

Secondly, Adam is also given responsibility to work in the Garden of Eden. In Genesis 2:15 he is told to 'work it and take care of it'. In this sense, work is to be understood as a blessing of Creation, not primarily as a curse of the Fall.

God giving work to Adam is sometimes referred to by theologians as the 'creation mandate', and some argue that it is reinforced throughout the Bible. An example of this emphasis occurs in Jeremiah's letter to the exiles in Babylon. In his letter, Jeremiah tells them to build houses, plant gardens to grow crops and to work for the prosperity of the city there (Jeremiah 29).

3. JESUS' LIFE ON EARTH

When Jesus came to live on earth as a human being (called the Incarnation) he came with a job to do. The life of Jesus begins the redemption and perfection of all of creation, which will be completed in the second coming of Christ. In John 5:17, Jesus declares, 'My Father is always at his work to this very day, and I, too, am working.'

4. THE CROSS AND THE RESURRECTION

After Jesus' death on the Cross, he was raised from the dead. His resurrected body was raised up from death with the same marks on it, and yet it was transformed and glorified (1 Corinthians 15:3-4). The Cross and the Resurrection are the beginning of the transformation of the world; our work is of inherent value, and like the rest of creation, will be perfected when Christ comes again.

In 1 Corinthians, at the end of a chapter dedicated to the Resurrection, Paul declares that 'your labour in the Lord is not in vain' (1 Corinthians 15:58). Therefore, the work we do on earth has lasting value.

5. JESUS' RETURN TO HEAVEN

Christ's Ascension to heaven shows us that the 'bridge' that we will cross is sound. Jesus' Ascension also means that he is seated at the right hand of the Father, and intercedes on our behalf. Therefore, when we pray in Jesus' name regarding work matters, we know that our prayers are heard and that they make a difference.

6. PENTECOST

Christ's promised gift of the Holy Spirit – which we have the privilege of receiving today, just as the early Christians did on the day of Pentecost (Acts) – provides the power we need to work out the purposes for which God has called us in our work.

KINGDOM WORK

The ministry of Jesus saw the Kingdom of God break into this world. The Kingdom of God may be defined as the 'sphere of God's goodness and rule' on the earth.

This Kingdom will not be fully realised until the second coming of Christ, and therefore has to be understood in terms of both the 'now' and the 'not yet'.

Our work is part of the expansion of God's Kingdom on earth, and as such, suffers from that same tension. That is why our work can seem to move between sometimes being fruitful and yet at other times being futile.

Dr Ravi Zacharias, the international evangelist, has described the purpose of mankind to be that of 'sonship' or 'daughtership' (that is, being in relationship with God as Father), 'worship' (giving honour and praise to God within that relationship), and 'stewardship' (responsibly stewarding the rest of creation).

Our work can touch all three of these areas. We are sons and daughters of God, who can work as stewards in a way that worships God, bringing him honour and praise. This is why we are told in Colossians 3:23, 'Whatever you do, work at it with all your heart, as working for the Lord.' It is of little surprise, therefore, to learn that the Hebrew word for 'work' (*avodah*) is the same word for 'worship'. Let us be able to say that our work-station is also our worship-station.

EXERCISE 2: WHY DO YOU WORK? (5 MINS)

This should be completed individually and then discussed in the small group.

In response to the question 'Why do you work?' tick the three answers that matter the most to you.

- to earn money and to enjoy life
- for personal satisfaction and success
- to bring about some social good
- to enjoy relationships and friendships with colleagues
- to evangelise and share my faith
- other (explain)

This exercise has no 'right' or 'wrong' answers. It is just to get you thinking about why you work. So, what is our God-given purpose in working?

PURPOSE

Jesus' work was aligned with that of his Father's, and he did what his Father had planned for him. We, too, need to identify the role that God has specifically called us to. When we do this, our work is infused with purpose.

There are various reasons (or purposes) why God may have placed you in your current job. Such as:

1. To be a responsible steward (note previous point on the inherent value of work itself)

2. To be a tent-maker – this is having a job that puts you in a place or position where you can do some missionary work

3. Earn money to give away to mission and the church

4. To earn your own money to support yourself and your family so that you are not a burden on others and their ministry (1 Thessalonians 4)

5. To be light in a dark place or to bring about change and a more godly way of working (see Jeremiah 48:11-12)

This could mean encouraging your company to consider Corporate Social Responsibility

6. To share the Good News about Jesus with your colleagues

7. To be a pastoral ear for your colleagues, etc

It is also important to remember that our primary responsibility at work is to do the job that we are being paid to do! When we do this to the best of our ability and with the utmost Christian integrity, then many other opportunities (such as evangelism) will probably follow. However, we are wrong when we think of these opportunities as the main focus of our working day. It does not honour God to spend all of our time trying to evangelise our colleagues when we are being paid to do our job!

TESTIMONY

Ask the person who has agreed to share their testimony to tell their story now. They should talk about their own experience of trying to discern God's purpose for their work. If you cannot find someone to speak, use the story from *God at Work*, pages 44–46.

HOLY JOBS

One of the biggest obstacles to Christians living out their faith in the workplace is the so-called 'sacred-secular divide'. This is reinforced by the inaccurate belief that some jobs are holy (such as being a Vicar or a full-time church worker) and others are not (such as being a shopkeeper, banker, policeman, etc).

We need to understand that if we are called into our particular job and go about it with the utmost Christian integrity then both bishops and bankers, nuns and nurses can have holy jobs!

Throughout scripture we find God's people involved in a vast array of different jobs: Abraham was a cattle trader; Joseph was Prime Minister and later dabbled in wheat futures; Luke was a doctor; the first Ethiopian convert was a central banker; Dorcas was in fashion; Simon the tanner was the Louis Vuitton of his day; and Jesus was, of course, a carpenter.

In his writings the apostle Paul uses the same word for manual labour as he does for Christian work. God is interested in every aspect of our work and draws no distinction between sacred and secular.

EXERCISE 3: GOD'S PURPOSE FOR OUR WORK (10 MINS)

(In small groups)

Ask the guests to discuss the following questions in their small groups, and pray together at the end about any issues or questions that come up.

- What is your job now; what is your current sphere of influence in it?
- What are you passionate about?
- What may God be calling you to do in the job you are currently in?
- Have you felt God speak to you about your job in the past?
- Pray for God to show you your purpose in your current job

CONCLUSION

Pray to close the session.

Father, we thank you for the example that you set for us in our own work. Thank you that you have a purpose for each of us at work. We pray that this week, while we are at work, you would use each of us as an effective tool for the advancement of your Kingdom. We ask that you would send your Holy Spirit to guide and inspire each one of us in what we do. In Jesus' name, Amen.

HOMEWORK/ GOING DEEPER

At home, pray through the questions in Exercise 3. Ask God to help you discern what he may be saying about your purpose in your current work situation.

SESSION 2

Ambition and Life Choices

PREPARE BEFOREHAND

- If you haven't done so already, please register your course online at godatwork.org.uk
- Before preparing their own talks, leaders can listen to a podcast of Ken Costa discussing the content of this session in an interview with Nicky Gumbel. For a full list of podcasts, please visit godatwork.org.uk/podcast
- Have some copies of What Color is Your Parachute? (Ten Speed Press, 2008) by Richard Bolles, or the Gallup Organisation's StrengthsFinder for guests to peruse or borrow
- Find someone to give their testimony (5 minutes). They should talk about a 'low point' in their career and the ways in which God helped them to persevere, in turn resulting in a positive outcome. Brief them before the session

INTRODUCTION

This session is about ambition and life choices. The word ambition elicits a mixed response.

In one of their songs the band, Radiohead said, 'Ambition makes you look pretty ugly.' The actor Johnny Depp said, 'Ambition has become a dirty word.' But, what does ambition mean for Christians?

If our ambition is aligned with what God has called us to do, then it can be a good thing, and we are right to ask his blessing in it. In God's grace and wisdom, he has chosen to work through us, the church, in extending his Kingdom in the world.

WHAT IS CHRISTIAN AMBITION?

Christian ambition can be defined as: 'The passionate and contented pursuit of challenging yet attainable God-given objectives.'

PASSIONATE

Roy Hattersley, in his biography of General Booth, *Blood and Fire: William and Catherine Booth and the Salvation Army* (Abacus, 2000), describes the 'reckless enthusiasm' that led Booth to form the Salvation Army. He was passionate about what he was called to do.

In Philippians, Paul writes, '...it is God who works in you to will and to act according to his good purpose' (Philippians 2:13).

Passion is equated with success. Jean Pierre Garnier, of GlaxoSmithKline, one of the world's largest pharmaceutical companies said this:

'I don't know anyone who is passionate and unsuccessful' (*Times 2*, 27 September 2005).

CONTENTED

Ambition should be contented. Contentedness comes from the knowledge that we are working for God in what he has called us to do. God gives us objectives that match our talents, or he provides the necessary gifts and skills required. The better we know ourselves and our talents, the more we can imagine what kind of work God might be calling us to. We are most contented at work when our gifts and talents are being used.

If you are unsure what your own strengths and talents are, you might like to try some analytical tools such as the book, *What Color is Your Parachute?* by Richard

Bolles, or the Gallup Organisation's *StrengthsFinder*.

CHALLENGING

Our ambitions should be challenging. The Revd John Collins said, 'Do not settle for black and white if God has given you a vision in colour.'

In Ken Costa's book, *God at Work*, Sir Terry Leahy, head of Tesco, has defined the challenge of leadership as follows:

Find out the truth of the situation, paint a picture of where you want to get to, make a plan and go and do it. Always believe that there is a better place and then persuade people to get there with you.

ATTAINABLE

Our ambitions should stretch us but they should also be attainable and achievable, or else we will lose belief in our purpose and lack momentum in what we are trying to do. Saying, 'One day when I am a billionaire, I'll give all my money to charity to feed millions of people' is a worthy sentiment, but is probably not what is meant by Christian ambition. Our ambitions need to challenge us but they also need to be attainable.

GOD-GIVEN

We need to know that our ambitions come from God and that he will give us what we need to complete them, as well as allowing him to step in and correct us when we go off-track. As we step out in faith to do his will, he will guide us.

Bearing all this in mind, **how do we make career choices?**

RELATIONSHIPS

Our main reference point when making decisions should be our relationship with God developed through regular prayer and reading the Bible. If we're not doing this on a regular basis, it's something we can begin to do more often, whether this means praying for ten minutes in the car on the way to work, reading in a park at lunchtime, or before we go to bed.

EXERCISE 1

This exercise aims to help us think about when we can read the Bible or pray during the day. Using the table in their manuals, ask guests to tick the times during the day when they could read the Bible or pray.

Time of day	Bible reading	Praying
Before breakfast		
Whilst running or at the gym		
Whilst commuting in the morning		
After the school run		
At my desk first thing		
During my lunch break		
Whilst commuting in the evening		
Before dinner		
After dinner		
With my partner just before bed		
In bed		
Other		

The psalmist writes 'The Lord confides in those who fear him; he makes his covenant known to them' (Psalm 25:14). We need to be asking God for guidance on a regular basis. This isn't to say that we should avoid our own responsibility. If we are asking God for an opportunity for a new job, we still need to fill in application forms. Asking for guidance is an interactive process that deepens our faith.

STEPPING OUT IN FAITH

However, making decisions is not always easy. Many of us, when faced with a choice, end up in paralysis; we just don't know what to do. It may be that this paralysis comes from the expectation that God will make our decisions for us (a passing of the buck), but we still need to act. It is often as we move forward and take the first step that we sense God's voice behind us saying, 'This is the way; walk in it' (Isaiah 30:21). God often expects us to make the first move. When sailing a boat, it is difficult to navigate while you are still in the dock. Once out of the harbour, you can feel the currents and the wind and set a course.

ADVICE FROM OTHERS

When we are faced with a career choice, such as whether to apply for a new role, accept a job offer, or go part-time, talking through the options with trusted, mature Christian friends can be an important part of the discernment process. This can also be a source of encouragement and support.

Additionally, God's timing is critical. As someone said, you cannot squeeze a fruit ripe. Isaiah 60:22 says, 'I am the Lord; in its time I will do this swiftly.' Sometimes we need to wait for God's timing before something happens.

If you no longer feel fulfilled or even 'called' to your current job, remember that we are not just called out of situations but into new openings and challenges. If we sense we are being called into something else, we should also experience a quickening of our spirit in a positive sense, an inclination towards another job, another sector, or another way of life. Paul tells us to, '...retain the place in life that the Lord has assigned you and to which God has called you' (1 Corinthians 7:17).

SIGNS

Signs are also an important part of decision making. In Judges 6:36-40 Gideon laid a fleece before the Lord to test a decision. It is important to note that the fleece was laid after the decision had been made, it was not a way of neglecting responsibility. Requests for signs, therefore, should be primarily confirmatory rather than predictive. For example, if you have applied for and been offered another job and you haven't yet resigned from your current position, you may want to ask God for a sign that it is right to leave.

TESTIMONY

At this point introduce the person who will share about a time in their life when they had a difficult, work-related decision to make. Ask them to talk about how God guided and helped them in this situation. If you can't find a suitable testimony, read out the story from *God at Work*, pages 61-63 (Pippa Richards, church worker).

HOW TO ACHIEVE YOUR AMBITIONS

So, how do we achieve our ambitions? It might sound obvious, but we need to start with the end in mind – in Isaiah 46:10, God declares, 'I make known the end from the beginning.'

In his diary (*The Diary of Soren Kierkegaard* (Citadel Press, 1998)), Soren Kierkegaard wrote, 'Life can only be understood backwards; but it must be lived forwards.'

Stephen Covey, in his book *The Seven Habits of Highly Effective People* (Simon & Schuster Ltd, 2004) urges us to start with the end in mind. He writes, 'If the ladder is not leaning against the right wall, every step we take gets us to the wrong place faster.'

In short, we need to know where we are going. It can help to split your long-term goals into shorter-term ones – this helps to break what can appear to be the impossible into smaller steps. Each little objective achieved will build morale and belief in the long-term goal. As you make steady progress along the way, you will build confidence to help you deal with the inevitable setbacks.

In Deuteronomy 7:22-23, Moses speaks about The Promised Land, 'The Lord your God will drive out those nations before you, little by little. You will not be allowed to eliminate them all at once, or the wild animals will multiply around you. But the Lord your God will deliver them over to you.'

With God, everything works together for good (Romans 8:28) and setbacks can become the springboards for achievement.

Some of us may need to change our mindset when faced with challenges. Sometimes what seems like a brick wall before us can just be a wall of papier-mâché. Often a change of mindset can be what is required to run straight through the wall.

Romans 12:2 is a challenge to us in this area: 'Do not conform any longer to the pattern of this world, but be transformed by the renewing of your mind. Then you will be able to test and approve what God's will is—his good, pleasing and perfect will.'

EXERCISE 2

The purpose of this exercise is to find out what motivates us at work.

Ask guests to put the motivations listed below in order between 1 and 10 related to what drives them to do well at work, with 1 being what drives them the most, and 10 being what drives them the least.

Guests should share their answers with another person.

- Service
- Money
- Promotion
- Status / Recognition
- Fulfilment
- Challenge
- Competition
- Winning
- Success
- Teamwork
- Other (describe)

Ask the group to do the exercise individually and then discuss their answers with their small group.

This exercise will have helped us to recognise what motivates us. We can all be motivated by good and bad things, so how do we recognise when our ambition is in the wrong areas?

DESTRUCTION AND DECEPTION
– HOW TO RECOGNISE THE DANGERS

Lives can be destroyed by ambition that gets out of control.

When our ambition becomes separated from the context of extending God's kingdom and our role in that, it risks destroying us. We need to remember that 'the heart is deceitful above all things' (Jeremiah 17:9).

If we are to avoid self-deception and hold our ambition lightly, we need to ask the Holy Spirit to show us our true intentions and we need to be accountable to those around us whom we know and trust.

Ask the guests to complete Exercise 3 in their manuals.

EXERCISE 3: THE 'AMBITION AUDIT'

Exercise 3 can help guests recognise if their ambitions are destructive. Guests should complete the 'Ambition Audit' by ticking one answer for each of the questions given.

	Agree strongly	Agree	Neither agree nor disagree	Disagree	Disagree strongly
Are you suspicious of others at work?					
Are you satisfied when others fail?					
Do you like talking about/ gossiping about others?					
Do you find it hard to receive advice from other people?					
Do you feel that you know best about your own ambition?					
I am not satisfied with my current job					

Now add up your score.

Score:

5 points for every 'Agree strongly' answer
4 points for every 'Agree' answer
3 points for every 'Neither agree nor disagree' answer
2 points for every 'Disagree' answer
1 point for every 'Disagree strongly' answer

Results

Score 30 to 21 – you may be gripped by a degree of selfish ambition.

Score 20 to 16 – a generally healthy attitude to ambition, but no room for complacency.

Score 15 to 6 – it is likely that you currently have no problems with selfish ambition.

If we are not sure if our ambitions are from God, the following questions can be helpful pointers for career direction:

1. Do I have confidence whilst praying and worshipping that God is setting the agenda or are there persistent niggles?
2. Is my ambition so personal that I don't want to talk about it with others?

When our ambitions align with God's will for our lives and our place in extending his kingdom, we will be content.

CONCLUSION AND PRAYER

Finally, commitment and perseverance (the ability to stick at the job we are called to do) are in short supply today. When we struggle and go through difficult situations we can be tempted to give up.

PERSEVERANCE

We all need discipline and perseverance in pursuing our God-given ambitions. Jesus is our ultimate example, and he was ambitious to complete the work that God had sent him to do (John 4:34). His last cry on the cross was, 'It is finished' (John 19:30). He completed the task he had been set to the very end, even in intense pain and suffering.

In the New Testament we read that the apostle Paul strained towards the goal God had given him. In the end he could say that he had 'fought the good fight' and had 'finished the race' (2 Timothy 4:7).

To end pray in small groups about the issues that have been raised in this session.

PRAYER POINT SUGGESTIONS

Some may feel they cannot see the purpose in their work and may want to pray about that. Others may be feeling tired and want to pray for strength to help them persevere in their work.

HOMEWORK/ GOING DEEPER

At home, spend some time thinking and praying about the following questions:

- What are your long-term goals for work?
- How can you split them into shorter-term goals?
- Spend time reassessing your own calling, and asking yourself if your ambitions are truly aligned with the purpose that God has given you
- If you know that you find it difficult to persevere, think about how you might increase your own perseverance in the right job

EXERCISE 4

Why do we sometimes find it hard to stick at the job that we have been called to? Ask guests to fill in the grid below ticking the degree to which each statement applies to them.

Reason	Applicability None	Applicability Low	Applicability Medium	Applicability High
Boredom/ Monotony				
Can't see purpose in it				
Burnt out/ tired				
Difficult relationships at work				
Don't feel competent at job				
Find it hard to live out faith at work				
Performance targets always set too high to meet				
Other reason(s)				

SESSION 3

Tough Decisions

PREPARE BEFOREHAND

- If you haven't done so already, please register your course online at godatwork.org.uk
- Before preparing their own talks, leaders can listen to a podcast of Ken Costa discussing the content of this session in an interview with Nicky Gumbel. For a full list of podcasts, please visit godatwork.org.uk/podcast
- Testimony slot – find someone to share a story of a time when they faced a moral or ethical decision at work and how they dealt with it

EXERCISE 1 (5 MINS)

Ask guests to identify one tough decision they have made in the past that was related to a work situation. How did they go about making the decision? What steps were taken before deciding what to do? These answers should be discussed with the rest of the small group.

We all make decisions in different ways. Some of us are impulsive, making decisions quickly and easily, others of us take longer and like to think through all the options. But how do we make decisions?

More often than not, decision-making is a process. There are four aspects to decision-making that can help us.

INTRODUCTION

We all are faced with tough decisions from time to time, in our home lives and especially at work. This session looks at a biblical framework for making tough decisions.

We're going to start this session with an exercise to get us thinking about how we make decisions.

1. SCRIPTURE

The Bible provides the framework for our actions. In other words, it gives us guidelines for how we should live. Our decisions should be aligned with what we are taught in Scripture.

2. REASON

Using our God-given faculties of reasoning. As Isaiah declared: 'Come now, let us reason together' (Isaiah 1:18). Using our common sense to work through the decision with others helps us work out what to do.

3. CONSCIENCE

What St Augustine called 'a kind of silent clamour of truth ringing inside.' The Holy Spirit guides us through our conscience. Sometimes a course of action feels 'right' and peaceful – this is our conscience prodding us in a God-ward direction.

4. CONSEQUENCES

We cannot make decisions in isolation. Our choices affect others as well as ourselves. When deciding whether to take a job overseas for example, we need to think about our family, not just our career prospects.

The best decisions are made when these four aspects are aligned.

DECISIONS AND VALUES

Integrity means that our decisions should be aligned with our values. We cannot compartmentalise our faith and our worklife. Rather we must align them, having integrity in every aspect of our work.

EXERCISE 2 (15 MINS)

The following exercise should be done in small groups.

Firstly, guests should individually identify one tough decision they are currently facing, but which they have not made yet. (If they are not facing a tough decision at present, guests should think about a potential issue that may come up in the future instead.) Guest should:

- Try to 'make the complex simple' by writing down the issue using the minimum amount of words possible
- Consider the four aspects – Scripture, Reason, Conscience and Consequences. Consider how each of these speak to the situation you are facing
- Think about how they might make the best decision in light of the above

Ask guests to discuss each aspect of making the decision with their small groups and pray for God's guidance as they go forward.

TESTIMONY

Invite the person who has agreed to tell their story to begin now. They should talk about a time when they faced a moral or ethical decision at work and how they dealt with this. If you cannot find anyone, use the story on pages 72-73 of *God at Work* (Alex Lee, finance director).

HOW TO MAKE WISE CHOICES

We will all face dilemmas and tough decisions at work from time to time. In certain circumstances we may face possible conflict. What should we do?

Sometimes it may be right to avoid conflict (in Luke 4:28-30, Jesus walked through the crowd, instead of arguing with them). Other times it may be wise to 'cut a deal' (Daniel 1:3-16). Occasionally, it may be right to take a stand (Daniel 3).

It can be helpful to consider theoretically what you would do in various situations so that you are prepared. In light of this, we come to the next exercise.

EXERCISE 3 (10 MINS)

Ask the groups to discuss the following case study (in their manual). Ask them to discuss what they would do in this situation.

'You've been asked to give a presentation to the boss of your boss on the project that your team is currently working on. The project requires investment from the business in order to survive and for the team to continue. You do some thorough research and predict the amount of business that you think the project will deliver. Your boss sees the projections before the presentation, and although he is impressed by your research, says the size of the project is not big enough and tells you to double the numbers. What do you do?'

After 5 minutes, get the group back together and explain that you are going to read Daniel 1:3-16 to see how Daniel faced a similar challenge. Start by explaining the background:

The background to this story is that the Babylonians had occupied Israel and taken a large part of the population (Israelites) to Babylon as exiles. Young, talented Israelites were selected for training to serve in the court of the King of Babylon. Daniel was one such young man. These men were to be given food and drink from the King's own table to make them strong, but to Jews like Daniel, this food was seen as 'unclean' and would compromise their religious beliefs. What should Daniel do?

Read Daniel 1:3-16

Discuss how Daniel went about a similar challenge.

Daniel made a wise decision. So, how can we do the same? We're going to look at five steps for making wise choices.

1. LISTEN TO THE QUESTION

In our jobs we have to deal with a range of questions every day. Some are small, some require more thought. What can we learn from the range of questions that Jesus faced?

i. In Luke 20:2, Jesus is asked by what authority he was doing things. He replies by asking his questioners whether John's baptism was from heaven or of human origin (Luke 20:3-4). They answer evasively saying, 'We don't know' (Luke 20:7), and Jesus therefore declines to answer their question. Jesus teaches us here that not every question has to be answered.

ii. Later on in the same chapter in Luke 20:21-22, Jesus is asked whether it is right to pay taxes to Caesar. His response in verse 25 shows us that just because we may be presented with a question with an extreme option of the questioner's own choice, we do not have to restrict our answers to the options offered.

iii. Finally, in Luke 20:27-33, the Sadducees ask a difficult but honest question about a woman with seven husbands. Jesus gives a clear and helpful reply. We can learn from this that when the real purpose of the question is to elicit a straight answer, then one should be given.

2. MAKE THE COMPLEX SIMPLE

Try to reduce the difficult decision to its simplest form. It helps to write down the issue using the minimum number of words. Simple choices are at the root of most complex decisions. For example, 'If I made this decision I will lose X in the short-term but gain Y in the long-term.' Simplifying the decision can help us see it for what it really is.

These choices can include moral elements that need consideration. In the words of General Omar Bradley, 'We have become a nation of technological giants and moral pygmies' (*God at Work*, Ken Costa).

3. FOLLOW THE WISDOM OF GOD

Wisdom is knowing and doing what is right and what comes from God. It is the art of living skilfully in whatever conditions we find ourselves. Daniel followed the wisdom of God.

When facing a critical choice or important decision our first response should be to step back and take time to see the situation from all angles. If you can, try to take two days out (perhaps over a weekend) to seek God.

Day one should be to rest and relax. Churning over an important decision can be very draining. Use day two – not to think over the issue again – but to meditate on who God is, on his ways and his overall plans for his people and for you. Focusing on God, rather than on the decision in hand, widens our perspective; this in turn will inform our decision.

4. CONSIDER THE CONSEQUENCES

The ability to make a wise decision can sometimes be destroyed by 'short-termism' (that is, not looking far enough ahead). It can be wise to take a long view. For example, when making a career decision, think about where each of the options will get you in five or ten years time.

We need to make tough decisions in the light of future, long-term circumstances. Jesus encourages us to think ahead in Luke 14:28 when he says, 'Suppose one of you wants to build a tower. Will he not first sit down and estimate the cost to see if he has enough money to complete it?'

When making a decision we should assess the risk. Too much time can be spent thinking about the potential benefits of a decision, when really it is the potential cost of things going wrong that needs the most careful attention. The hope is that we might have peace in the decision, as seen Isaiah 26:3:

'You will keep in perfect peace him whose mind is steadfast, because he trusts in you' (Isaiah 26:3).

Ask for advice from trusted friends who know you well. Sharing a difficult decision you are facing with a couple of wise, spiritually mature friends can give perspective and provide support. Pray with them and ask God to speak through them, or to confirm that which you have already begun to discern.

5. IMPLEMENT THE STRATEGY

As Christians we are called to be 'as shrewd as snakes and as innocent as doves' (Matthew 10:16). We read about an example of this in Daniel 1, as discussed earlier in the session. When Daniel was taken to the Babylonian court, he resolved not to defile himself with the non-kosher food and wine from the King's table. But rather than flatly refusing, Daniel made a pragmatic suggestion to the chief

official of a ten day trial period of just eating vegetables. At the end of it, Daniel and his friends looked so healthy, they got what they wanted.

CONCLUSION AND PRAYER

End the session with a short time of prayer.

PRAYER POINT SUGGESTIONS

Some people may feel that they have made unwise decisions recently, while others may be facing a tough decision in the near future; both situations require prayer.

HOMEWORK/ GOING DEEPER

Think about your values. List three or four values that you would like to live by consistently, both in and out of the workplace. Share these with another person and pray for God's help to live them out.

SESSION 4

Stress and Work-Life Balance

PREPARE BEFOREHAND

- If you haven't done so already, please register your course online at godatwork.org.uk
- Before preparing their own talks, leaders can listen to a podcast of Ken Costa discussing the content of this session in an interview with Nicky Gumbel. For a full list of podcasts, please visit godatwork.org.uk/podcast
- Testimony slot – find someone who can share how one or more of the seven biblical strategies have helped them deal with stress
- Books – Have some copies of Psalms for People Under Pressure (The Athlone Press, 2004) by Jonathan Aitken to show

INTRODUCTION

Welcome to the fourth session of the *God at Work* course. This session deals with stress and work-life balance. Of all the lifestyle issues we face today, stress is the most prevalent. It is a national health problem in many countries.

Across many areas of our lives, there is an increasing pressure for us to take on more than we can manage; this is especially true at work. How often have you heard yourself say 'I haven't got enough time!'? How does our faith affect how we view our work-life balance and how we cope with stress?

When you hear the term 'work-life balance', what comes to mind?

IMPLICATIONS OF STRESS

The implications of stress are huge. It affects us in many ways, including medically. Two hundred men were monitored over ten years for the 'Work Site Blood Pressure Study', published in the *American Journal of Epidemiology*.

The study revealed that stress at work puts the same strain on the heart as being forty pounds overweight and that prolonged bouts of tension have the same effect on blood pressure as ageing thirty years. Those who suffer stress often have trouble sleeping or report waking up in the night worrying about work.

Stress also produces a range of psychological side effects, most notoriously an inability to concentrate for a sustained period of time. Those who suffer from stress may find themselves inundated with irrational fears or aggression towards colleagues. When we are stressed we may feel overwhelmed; when we are not working we may feel guilty.

Stress can affect us spiritually, too. It can destroy perspective, make us self-absorbed and prevent us from seeing the bigger picture. It can strangle our relationships with other people, as well as with God.

In the parable of the sower (Mark 4:1–20), we read about how some seed grows at first, only to be 'choked' by the thorns and weeds that represent the worries and desires of this world. It can feel like stress chokes various aspects of our lives, particularly our relationships.

Stress also affects us economically. In the UK alone, 13 million working days are lost due to stress every year.

FOOLISH APPROACHES

There are several foolish ways to approach stress. The first is to deny it exists. Sadly, this approach simply stores it up, only for the implications stated above to erupt at a later stage.

The second is to pretend that stress is good. Some colleagues wear it as a 'badge of honour', to try and prove that they are working really hard for the company. There was even a management course in the early 1990s entitled 'The Joy of Stress'!

STRESS VS PRESSURE

It is important to note that stress and pressure are not the same. Stress is our own adverse reaction to excessive pressure. We can adopt a 'twin approach', trying either to influence the external pressures placed upon us, or trying to influence the way we react internally to these pressures.

EXERCISE 1: WHAT IS MOST STRESSFUL ABOUT YOUR JOB? (5 MINS)

As this session starts, guests should share in their small groups their answers to the question 'What is most stressful about your job?' Also ask guests to decide where they would put themselves at the moment on the 'Pressure/Performance Curve'. The graph shows our level of performance at work in relation to the level of pressure we face.

THE PRESSURE/PERFORMANCE CURVE

Performance

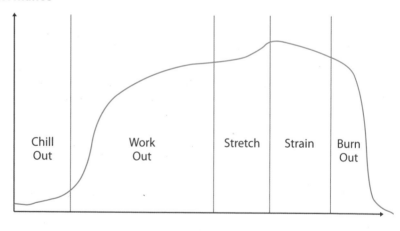

Level of Pressure

The first part of the session is going to look at the internal approach to stress. The second part will look at the external approach.

I. INTERNAL APPROACH

This approach focuses on how we can limit any adverse, internal reaction we may have to the external pressure that we face.

Any approach to dealing with stress should begin by remembering that Jesus understands and has experienced incredibly stressful days. The garden of Gethsemane is one example, as is the day recorded in Luke 8:22-56.

So how do we deal with stress?

SEVEN BIBLICAL STRATEGIES

1. STAY HEALTHY

1 Corinthians 6:19 tells us that our body is a temple of the Holy Spirit. Eating well and allowing time in our week for exercise can help us wind down and stay healthy.

2. PRAY AND READ THE BIBLE

This may seem obvious, but it is the most important of all the strategies. Praising God should be our weapon of first resort, as it lifts us to that higher, eternal perspective. Paul encourages us to pray at all times in Philippians 4:6, and stresses the importance of knowing the Scriptures in 2 Timothy 3:15-17.

3. FIGHT FEAR

Psalm 112:7 states that those who trust 'will have no fear of bad news; their hearts are steadfast, trusting in the Lord.' When we are in a stressful situation we can ask God for the peace of the Holy Spirit (John 14:27).

4. TAKE JOY SERIOUSLY

In 1 Thessalonians 5:16 Paul commands the Thessalonians to 'be joyful always.'

5. TAKE AN EMOTIONAL BREAK

This may be as simple as sending an email that is unrelated to work at a time of intense stress (if you are able to do this), or deciding not to talk about work when you are having one-to-one time with your spouse. Worshipping together can be a great way of having an emotional break from pressure. Jesus often withdrew for 'mini-breaks' throughout his ministry, an example of this can be found in in John 6:15. Rick Warren talks about 'diverting daily, withdrawing weekly and abandoning annually.'

6. TAKE CONTROL OF OUR THOUGHTS

Philippians 4:8 tells us to focus on whatever is true, right, noble, pure, etc. This is important, because when we are stressed our thoughts can become very negative and spiral downwards. As Christians we are to be transformed by the renewing of our minds.

We need to develop an abundance mentality instead of a 'scarcity mentality'. The latter says that there is never enough; either God is not enough, or he is not interested in our problems. The former says that the God who has prepared every good work for us is also an eternal, all-powerful, loving God.

7. MINISTER IN THE OPPOSITE SPIRIT

This is the spiritual equivalent of counting to ten. When colleagues criticise our work, we should seek to complement them on theirs, rather than becoming stressed about their critical attack on ours. The apostle Paul continually ministered in the opposite spirit, as we are told by him in 1 Corinthians 4:12-13.

Admiral Lord Nelson of the British Navy observed and recorded the weather twice a day, every day of his life. This meant that he could predict the storm that would occur three days before the battle of Trafalgar when he faced the combined French and Spanish fleets. He devised his daring strategy for the battle around the assumption that the storm would break. It did, and he won the battle, although his fleet was outnumbered.

When we read the Bible every day, it may seem mundane at times, but we never know when we will need to call on it to help us through a stressful time.

TESTIMONY

Invite the person who has agreed to tell their story to begin now. They should talk about a time when one (or more) of the seven biblical strategies helped them to deal with stress. If you cannot find anyone, use the story on pages 125-126 of *God at Work* (Anita Patel, physiotherapist) about ministering in the opposite spirit.

II. EXTERNAL APPROACH: ACHIEVING WORK-LIFE BALANCE

This brings us to the second part of the session, looking at the external approach to dealing with stress.

Another approach to dealing with stress is to try to influence the external pressures placed upon us.

PREVENTATIVE

Work-life balance begins with setting the right priorities. Most Christians agree that the order of priorities in our life should be: God first, followed by our core relationships and then work. Getting sufficient rest is also important. We need to respect the Sabbath, even if not legalistically, by taking a day each week to rest.

Isaiah 28:11-13 speaks of the foolish state of Ephraim in not taking this time to rest.

MANAGING TIME OR PRIORITIES?

People often say, 'I don't have enough time.' But the truth is that we manage priorities not time.

Time itself is a constant, we cannot influence it – as Arnold Bennett remarked in his book, *How to Live on 24 Hours a Day*, 'We shall never have more time. We have, and always have had, all the time there is.'

It can help to remember that when it comes to timing, God knows the bigger picture. In John 11:1–16, Jesus waited two days upon hearing of Lazarus' illness before leaving to visit him. Although that meant that Lazarus died, Jesus knew that God would be glorified by the raising of Lazarus.

COMPULSIONS AND ADDICTIONS

Various things can work to twist the way we prioritise. Compulsions and addictions are two of these, and we're going to spend some time looking at them in the next exercise. We can be slaves to habits and attitudes that affect the way we live.

EXERCISE 2

Ask guests to fill out the grid by ticking the box that shows the extent to which each issue applies to their lives. They should share the top issue with someone in their small group.

Bad habit / Attitude	Applicability None	Applicability Low	Applicability Medium	Applicability High
Workaholism				
Lust for money				
Unforgiveness				
Anger				
Lying				
Substance abuse				
Pornography				
Eating extremes				
Unfaithfulness				
Power seeking				
Identity in appearance				
Identity in being in relationships				
Identity in consuming (shopping/ materialism)				
Irrational fear				
Other (describe)				

IDOLS

Idols are anything that push God out of our lives. Only God can break the power of destructive habits and bring balance to our lives. Workaholism can be as acute an addiction as any recreational substance. Workaholics often rely on work to give meaning to life, and the root cause of the issue sometimes lies in childhood, where they were under pressure to achieve in order to 'earn' gratification.

At Jesus' baptism, his Father declares that Jesus is his son, whom he loves (Luke 3:22). It is after his baptism that Jesus' ministry began. Here we can see that unconditional love should precede work, not vice versa.

If we have a bad habit in our life, then one prayer might demolish it, but usually we need to lay siege to it, and persistently ask God to dismantle it over time.

FREEDOM AND DISCIPLINE – HOW TO GET THE TREND LINE RIGHT?

The short-term breakdown of time spent between work, family and God is not important, rather it is the longer-term trend that matters.

We all go through periods when work might demand longer hours than usual, or when we need to invest more time in the family (for example when a new baby arrives). However, it is our long-term trend that most accurately reveals our priorities.

There is an exercise in the homework, which allows you to plot how your time has been divided between working, being with your family and being with God/involved with church over the past year.

DIARY REVIEWS

There are several ways of ensuring that we are prioritising our time the way we feel is right. The first is to conduct an annual diary review.

You may wish to put a date in the diary for this now! The diary review should look back at the past year and work out how your time has been divided between work, family and God. After the review, plan your forward diary for the next year, making sure it reflects your chosen lifestyle and priorities.

Within this forward plan, make sure you allow for flexibility. Schedule some 'spare' time, in case the unexpected happens.

LIFE REVIEWS

A life review is wider than a diary review, and can be helpful when you wish to consider your call and purpose in life. Life reviews should be infrequent, taking place at key moments in your life. Fast and pray as you consider these bigger questions.

Remember that if God calls us out of one career, then it is to call us into another. If we feel disillusioned with our current job, then it might just be the frustration of being in a 'middle patch'.

CONCLUSION AND PRAYER

You may wish to end this session with a corporate time of repentance and prayer in light of anything that has come up in the exercise on bad habits and attitudes.

PRAYER POINT SUGGESTIONS

Conclude the session by sharing in the small groups about what has been most relevant for you this session. Pray in the small group about any issues that have been raised.

HOMEWORK/ GOING DEEPER

Use the blank graph to plot an estimate of how your time has been divided between working, being with your family and being with God/ involved with church over the past year. An example is filled in to show you what to do.

Then consider what you would like the trend lines to be.

Spend some more time praying about the right priorities for your life. Conduct an official diary review and prayerfully plan your diary for the next year, ensuring it reflects your future priorities.

Example pie-chart

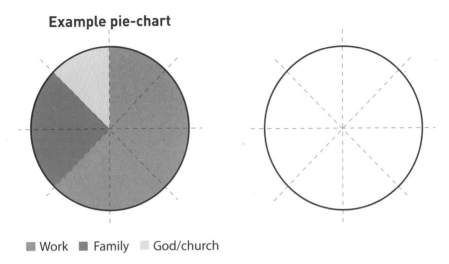

■ Work ■ Family ■ God/church

VERSES FOR MEDITATION IN TIMES OF STRESS

Psalm 46   Matthew 6:25-34

Isaiah 43:1-3   Philippians 4:6-7

SESSION 5

Failure, Disappointment and Hope

PREPARE BEFOREHAND

- If you haven't done so already, please register your course online at godatwork.org.uk
- Before preparing their own talks, leaders can listen to a podcast of Ken Costa discussing the content of this session in an interview with Nicky Gumbel. For a full list of podcasts, please visit godatwork.org.uk/podcast
- Testimony slot – find someone who can share their experience of how God helped them recover from disappointment or failure at work; ask them to mention how he renewed their hope

INTRODUCTION

The subjects of this session are failure, disappointment and hope.

Everyone experiences failure and disappointment. It would be unusual if we did not experience disappointment in our working lives; we may be overlooked for a promotion, or we may be made redundant.

We may fail to secure a deal or reach a target; a colleague may betray us or let us down, or we may make a mistake and be filled with shame.

EXERCISE 1: FAILURE

Ask the group to share examples of failure that they have experienced in the workplace.

We all suffer failure and disappointment in our personal and work lives.

How is it possible to find hope and deal with failure and disappointment?

FAITH AND ETERNITY

The source of Christian hope arises from the knowledge that we are made by a God who loves each one of us. Romans 5:5 says this:

'And hope does not disappoint us, because God has poured out his love into our hearts by the Holy Spirit, whom he has given us.'

Christian hope is not mere optimism. Nor is it having hope in our own desires and asking God to bless those desires. Instead, Christian hope is based on a relationship with God, through faith. The Bible tells us that God has invested in our lives, marking us with a sign (or seal) of his ownership. The Holy Spirit is like a 'deposit' we have been given in this life that guarantees the full payment later. We are utterly secure in this life because Christ has underwritten his investment in us. Our lives have eternal value, and we have eternal hope.

Jesus died on the cross to take our sin. Essentially, he gave us his riches for our poverty. Every day we can ask God to take our guilt, mistakes and failures and exchange them for peace, security and purpose. This relates to our time at work as much as any other area of our lives.

FORGIVENESS AND RESTORING RELATIONSHIPS

It is vital that we build good relationships with our work colleagues; we may spend more time with them than with our family or friends. Good working relationships will not only make our lives easier, but will also fulfil Christ's call to 'live at peace with everyone' (Romans 12:18).

To maintain good relationships with our colleagues, we need to learn to say sorry and to practise forgiveness in the workplace. We need to be people of **grace** (as modelled by Christ), **truth** (often a tradable commodity in the workplace), and **trust** (without trust the free market is endangered).

When trust is broken, we must learn to trust again. Reconciliation is at the heart of faith and this pushes us, often against our instincts, to begin to rebuild trust. Mutual trust is drawn from the example of the Trinity.

HOW DO WE REBUILD TRUST WHEN IT HAS BEEN BROKEN?

All of us probably have memories of broken relationships at work. Perhaps our idea was taken by someone else and passed off as his or her own. Maybe someone lied to you, or you may have been let down at the last minute of a crucial project by someone who didn't have an excuse.

At some time or another, we may think or say, 'I just can't trust that person ever again', but the reality is that we still need to work together. So how do we rebuild trust?

We need God to help us have the grace to make peace, even when we don't feel like it. In these situations it is important to approach the other person, although it can be a good idea to wait between twenty-four and fourty-eight hours to allow emotions to cool down. Then, have a frank discussion. There is no lasting value in not being upfront about the facts, but try to be calm and gracious as you speak. We can't expect things to be back to normal straight away following the discussion, but we can forgive and move on. Apologising where we have been in the wrong and forgiving those who have hurt us in the workplace both go a long way to rebuilding trust.

EXERCISE 2: IDENTIFYING BROKEN TRUST (10 MINS)

This first exercise aims to identify any relationships at work where trust has been broken. In the small groups, guests should ask themselves the following questions and then share their answers with the group. There will be time to pray through any issues that arise at the end of the session.

- What have I failed to do that I should be doing?
- What have I done (or am I doing) that I should not do?
- What has the other person done, or failed to do?
- What has been said that has been hurtful?

PAIN – WHAT CAN IT TELL US?

If we are to learn from the pain that we feel at work, we need to understand why we feel this way in the first place. Pain usually stems from:

- sin (ours or someone else's)
- being disciplined by the Father
- being pruned by the Son in order to bear more fruit, or
- being stirred by the Spirit to move on to something new

EXERCISE 3: LEARNING FROM FAILURE

This exercise is an opportunity to list any recent failures at work and assess what we can learn from them, as well as what could be done differently next time. Ask guests to fill in the table below, listing any recent failures. Responses to the questions should be written in the table.

Failure	What can I learn from it?	What would I do differently next time?

FAILURE – AN OPPORTUNITY TO GROW!

At some point, it is inevitable that we will all fail at work. However, if a project we are working on fails, this does not mean that we are failures as people. Although it can be difficult, we must try not to allow a chain of negative emotions to be set off.

We must remember that we are only failures if Christ fails in us – and he will never do that. We can be confident that 'he who began a good work in [us] will carry it on to completion' (Philippians 1:6).

In all aspects of life it can be helpful to honestly acknowledge our failures and learn from them. In John 21 we read about the disciples who have been out all night fishing. When asked about their catch they are honest enough to say, 'We have no fish.' However, they still trust Jesus' ability to turn things around. When they follow his instruction to fish on the right side, their nets are filled to bursting (John 21:6).

Failure can also go a long way in developing our characters. For example, failing at something can help kill pride and develop humility. Thus, God can use it even if he does not cause it – God promises to work in all things for the good of those who love him (Romans 8:28).

HOW TO RECOVER AND RENEW OUR HOPE

So how can we recover our hope?

Siegmund Warburg said, 'Some name it disappointment and become poorer, others name it experience and become richer.'

Let's look at five steps to recover and renew our hope.

1. TURN TO GOD (RATHER THAN IMPLICATE HIM IN THE FAILURE)

The disciples on road to Emmaus were so preoccupied with disappointment they failed to recognise the Lord of hope walking alongside them.

Jesus has promised never to abandon us (Matthew 28:20).

2. FACE THE FACTS, YET STILL BELIEVE

In the story of Abraham and Sarah, they longed for a child. We read of how Abraham acknowledged how old he and Sarah were (he faced the facts), yet he still believed and trusted in God's promise (Romans 4:19).

3. MEDITATE ON SCRIPTURE LED BY THE SPIRIT (ROMANS 15:13)

The Bible is the Word of God, and when we ask the Spirit to guide us, God speaks through his word.

The Bible is full of God's promises to us and his assurance that we can put our hope in him. Meditating on his word helps reinforce our hope.

4. KEEP A JOURNAL

A prayer journal can be an effective way to record your thoughts and prayers regularly. The act of writing our thoughts, feelings and prayers serves to help us express what we are feeling to God.

Written words often have a more objective ring to them – sometimes the act of writing helps us work out what we feel or think about a certain situation.

A journal can also be reviewed at a later date, when we are often able to see how God has worked in a situation. This builds our faith.

5. PERSEVERE IN HOPE (IT LEADS TO CHARACTER NOT DISAPPOINTMENT)

We read that perseverance leads to hope, and that hope does not disappoint us.

TESTIMONY

Invite the person who has agreed to give their testimony to begin now. Ask them to talk about a time when God helped them recover from disappointment or failure at work, in turn renewing their hope. If you cannot find a suitable story, use the one from *God at Work*, on pages 146–147 (Roger Philip, self-employed).

CONCLUSION AND PRAYER

To end the session, discuss what has been most relevant for you this session and pray in small groups about any issues that came up in the first two exercises.

PRAYER POINT SUGGESTIONS

You may want to pray for those who have recently experienced failure, as well as for those wanting a new sense of hope and direction in their work.

HOMEWORK/ GOING DEEPER

Take some time to pray into any relationships at work where you know that forgiveness is required. Either alone, or with other members of the group, spend some time forgiving those people before God, and asking forgiveness for your part (if any) in the difficulty. Pray for God's blessing on all your work relationships going forward.

SESSION 6

Money and Giving

PREPARE BEFOREHAND

- If you haven't done so already, please register your course online at godatwork.org.uk
- Before preparing their own talks, leaders can listen to a podcast of Ken Costa discussing the content of this session in an interview with Nicky Gumbel. For a full list of podcasts, please visit godatwork.org.uk/podcast
- Testimony slot – find someone who can share about how God has blessed them (preferably not in a financial way) through exercising the habit of giving
- Exercise 2 involves identifying work in the church that guests would like to invest in. You may like to have some information available about possible ministries that need support
- Debt – the subject of this session is money and giving. There may be people on the course who are in difficult financial situations including debt. If possible, have some information on debt counselling available

INTRODUCTION

For most of us, one of the results of our work is the monthly pay cheque. Of course, money is not the only reward, but somehow it is viewed differently. We react differently to receiving money – sometimes positively, and sometimes negatively. We can't avoid money, it affects us all, whether we are rich, or whether we are struggling financially. The Bible speaks to all situations, and in this session we'll be looking at a biblical view of money and giving.

EXERCISE 1 (5 MINS)

From largest to smallest, guest should list the areas where their money goes.

Ask them to look at where giving to God and the church come in the list. Do they think this should be higher up?

In small groups, guests should discuss their answers to the questions.

As we begin, let's look at some basics about money.

WHAT IS MONEY FOR?

Firstly, what is money for?

- It is primarily a medium of exchange – that is, it is a means of buying things we need to live, such as food, transport, housing and to pay bills for services we need, such as water and electricity

It is also used as:

- A store of value (such as savings)
- A vehicle of blessing:
  › Giving money blesses the person who receives it, but also transfers to them the responsibility of deciding what to do with it. This is an opportunity for the receiver to grow and learn. (Just as when children are given pocket money.)
  › In terms of using money for blessing, Christians have a particular duty to the poor and to issues of social justice
- A test of stewardship – do we look after what we have or waste it?
- A means of worshipping God (if we honour him with our money)

- Testimony and witnessing about God (if we use our money in a godly way)
- For making friends (Luke 16:9) by investing in people and relationships
- For investing in the Kingdom of God (1 Timothy 6:19)

Haggai's description seems apt for our age: 'You eat, but never have enough. You drink, but never have your fill. You put on clothes, but are not warm. You earn wages, only to put them in a purse with holes in it' (Haggai 1:6).

JESUS OR MONEY – WHO WILL BE THE MASTER?

In Luke 16:13, when Jesus declares that you cannot be a slave to both God and money, he uses language that is relational in its vocabulary, using words such as 'hate' and 'love'. The key question that Jesus leaves us with is – will we have a relationship with God or money?

When we read the Bible we find a great deal of teaching about how to handle money.

Having money is not a bad thing,

but we need God's help to ensure that it does not become our master; God must remain our guide and our master. Being successful in the workplace due to a degree of personal motivation is okay. Jesus states in Luke 10:7 that 'the worker deserves his wages.' However, 1 Timothy 6:9–10 also warns that the love of money is a root of all kinds of evil. We need God's help to ensure that money does not drive us.

EXERCISE 2: SELF SEEKING OR SEEKING SENSE?

In small groups, ask guests to read through the table below together.

Guests should look at the four key distinctions between self seeking and seeking sense and discuss the differences between the two.

Self Seeking	Seeking Sense
Exclusive (Thinks of self at exclusion of others)	Inclusive (Thinking of self doesn't exclude thinking of others)
Excessive (Tendency to always want more)	Sufficient (Desires not necessarily excessive)
Restrictive (Finds it difficult to give)	Releasing (Giving may come easily)
Stifling (Finds it hard when others prosper)	Empowering (May help others to prosper)

Ask the groups to feedback any observations and acknowledge that the difference between the two can sometimes be a fine line.

A key test is that if we find giving difficult, rather than joyful, then money could well have become our master.

GREED OR GENEROSITY – HOW DO WE DEAL WITH MONEY?

The example of Luke 16:10-11 is an important one. First, if you handle small amounts of money properly, then you can be trusted with larger amounts. If you fiddle your expense claim or try to get away without paying for your bus fare, who will trust you with larger amounts of money?

Secondly, if you cannot handle money properly, who will trust you with true riches? The small ways in which we use our money determine the trust that can be placed in us, not only by other people but by God.

DUTY AND PRIVILEGE – WHY DO WE GIVE?

We give for various reasons. Firstly, grace. We have been shown extreme grace by God, and our material giving is just one small way in which we can pass on the blessing we have received from him.

Secondly, we give in and by faith. In Psalm 96:4 the Psalmist declares,

I will honour you 'above all gods.' We honour God above everything else, including money.

Thirdly, we give because giving is a blessing. Generous, regular giving is one of the ways in which we show that we trust in God. Money can become either an obstacle or a gateway to God's blessing (this blessing may well not be a financial blessing).

Giving is one of the great privileges we have and a practical way of responding to God's love. When we get our giving right the wonderful promise of God is this, 'Test me and see if I don't open up heaven itself to you and pour out blessings beyond your wildest dreams' (Malachi 3:10, The Message).

TESTIMONY

Invite the person who has agreed to share their testimony to begin now. Ask them to tell the group how God has blessed them (preferably not in a financial way) through exercising the habit of giving.

If you cannot find someone to share their testimony, then please use the following story as an example of God's blessing through giving:

A course leader from the UK shares this story as an example of how giving can be a blessing in more ways than one. 'When my wife and I first got married, we were given a car. It wasn't flash, but it was just what we needed. Eventually, we were able to get another car. My wife suggested that rather than have the luxury of two cars, we should give our old car away. We gave it to a girl who was just starting out as a youth worker. The car was a blessing for this girl, but the act of giving it away was also a real blessing for my wife and I. It made us aware that ultimately, all resources belong to God and all we do is look after them and then pass them on.'

WHAT SHOULD GIVING LOOK LIKE?

1. CELEBRATION

Giving should be a celebration of what we have been given from God. Paul, writing to encourage generosity in the Christians at Corinth, says, 'Because of the service by which you have proved yourselves, people will praise God' (2 Corinthians 9:13).

He also says 2 Corinthians 9:7 that, 'God loves a cheerful giver.' Bishop Sandy Millar used to encourage his congregation to indulge only in 'hilarious giving'.

2. FREEDOM

Every time we give, we issue a defiant statement to the forces that lie behind money, saying, in effect, 'you don't have a hold on me.'

Wealth can give us the illusion that we don't need God, that we can survive on our own. But this is a lie. We will be possessed by that which we cannot give freely. Giving is the antidote to materialism.

3. INVESTMENT

Investing in our relationship with God: giving is a central part of the process by which we become more like Christ. Giving is our planting and the harvest is our righteousness (2 Corinthians 9:10).

Investing in God's wider kingdom: as we give generously today, we are not only helping immediate need (such as hunger), but also investing for future generations

Philippians 4:17-18 makes it clear that the giving of the Philippians is a credit (not debit) to their account. It is the same for us.

SMALL GROUP DISCUSSION (3 MINS)

In small groups, ask guests to identify work in their churches which excites them and that they would like to invest in. Responses should be discussed with their small groups.

THE PRACTICALITIES OF GIVING

As we come to the end, let's look at some of the practical issues related to giving.

AS A HABIT

Giving is a habit. There are always good reasons to put it off, so it is important just to start. Even if you start small, just start, and the habit will grow. Jesus says, 'Give and it will be given to you... For with the measure you use, it will be measured to you' (Luke 6:38). We shouldn't expect that this will be dollar for dollar, rather blessing upon blessing.

TO WHOM SHOULD WE GIVE?

The lion's share should go to the church. There are lots of people who give to charities, but only Christians will give to the church. Investing in the church is a way of investing in the future spiritual life of our nations. It is important to build a relationship with that to which we give. That way we can know how it is being used and ensure we are being good stewards of it.

HOW SHOULD WE GIVE?

Giving should usually be anonymous – the left hand should not know what the right hand is doing (Matthew 6:3), although occasionally knowing the source of giving can demonstrate the body of Christ at work. Christ is honoured when the known needs of Christians are met by other Christians.

We can also give our time, skills, possessions, etc, through volunteering at the church. If we have a spare room in our house, we can offer it. If we have a car, we can insure someone else to drive it.

WHEN SHOULD WE GIVE?

Some impulse giving is good, but the Bible encourages regular giving (1 Corinthians 16:2). If we get into a habit, we will find it easier to give.

WHAT SHOULD WE GIVE?

Most of the New Testament focuses on our attitude in giving rather than on the quantity.

EXERCISE 3: WHAT CAN WE GIVE? (10 MINS)

Ask guests to list what they feel they should/can give in terms of time/possessions/skills, etc. They can share what they have written with their small groups. They should pray for each other, asking that they would have the grace to be generous givers and give as God guides you to.

DEBT

If someone is in bad debt (not meaning having a normal mortgage, but chronic financial crisis), getting out of debt as quickly as possible is probably the best way to honour God. If you are in this situation, talk to someone trustworthy to acknowledge the problem and to establish a plan to resolve it.

RESPONSIBLE ENJOYMENT OF POSSESSIONS

Giving frees us up to enjoy God's goodness precisely because our priorities are right. When we have the balance right, we'll be able to enjoy both what we have and what we give.

CONCLUSION

Money is a difficult area for all of us, and we need God's help to be generous givers. We're going to end the session with a time of prayer in our small groups.

HOMEWORK/GOING DEEPER

The following exercises can be used to go deeper in this issue.

ASSESS YOUR GIVING EXERCISE

Guests should take some time to re-assess their giving in terms of who, how, when and what. They should imagine the blank pie-charts in their manuals represent all the money and time that they give in a year. Ask them to divide up the pie-charts as they would like to divide up their giving. They will need to adjust any plans to give in the light of this assessment.

DIVIDING UP YOUR GIVING

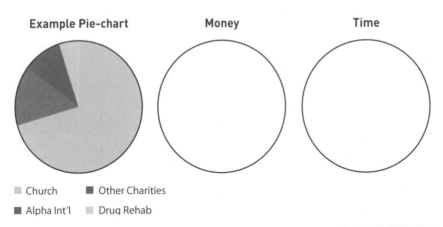

Example Pie-chart   Money   Time

■ Church   ■ Other Charities
■ Alpha Int'l   ■ Drug Rehab

THE 'SIX MONTH CHALLENGE'

Suggest growing in faith-based giving by taking up a six month challenge of either:

1. Reducing your discretionary spending by X%;
2. Increasing your giving by X%, or
3. Matching your luxury spending with equal giving
   (eg, if you buy a treat for yourself, give the equivalent amount away)

With your group, decide on a date (approximately six months from the challenge's start date) on which to meet together and discuss what God has done in your lives over that period.

FURTHER INFORMATION

For further information about *God at Work* please see: godatwork.org

We would love to hear your feedback on the course. Please tell us your thoughts online at: godatwork.org.uk

For the complete list of *God at Work* podcasts, please see: godatwork.org.uk/podcast

Alpha International publishes a wide range of resources for many different ministries. One of these ministries, Alpha in the Workplace, has developed a version of the Alpha course designed for use in a workplace setting. To learn more about this course, or to find out how to run one in your own workplace, please visit alpha.org/workplace

To find out more about the Alpha course, or to find a course near you, please visit alpha.org or alphafriends.org

To order *God at Work* resources, or any other Alpha International products, please visit:

- alphashop.org
- call the Alpha Publications Hotline on 0845 7581 278
- email alpha@stl.org
- to order products from overseas, please call + 44 1228 611 749